Journey Through NORTH AMERICA

Saronne Rubyan

HORUS EDITIONS

Horus Editions

Created and produced by Horus Editions

Series Editor
Elizabeth Miles
Copy-editor
Helen Maxey
Designers
Paul Richards, Richard Rowan
Cover design
David Till
Illustrators
Mike Bell, Jim Channell, Helen Parsley,
Martin Sanders, Gerald Witcomb

Author
Saronne Rubyan is a freelance writer and a schools'
learning support assistant. Saronne was born in
California and majored in English at Wayne State
University, Detroit, USA.

Consultant
Peter Ling BA (Hons), MA, PhD is Senior Lecturer
and Director of Undergraduate Studies in the School
of American and Canadian Studies at the University of
Nottingham, England.

Published by Horus Editions
Award Publications Limited
1st Floor, 27 Longford Street
London NW1 3DZ

Copyright © 2000 Horus Editions

A CIP catalogue record of this book is available from
the British Library.

ISBN 1-899762-32-9

Printed in Belgium

THE
JOURNEY

In the pages of this book we go on an incredible journey across the continent of North America. Our route takes us from the east to the west coast, and back again, through bustling cities, dusty deserts, across mighty rivers and through mysterious swamps. Highlights include a Native American pow-wow, a trip into Death Valley, and a flight over the Grand Canyon.

We travel by coach, boat, train, helicopter and aeroplane, and even take a short ride in a limousine. We visit many different peoples along the way and see some fascinating creatures. Don't miss the monster lizard, alligators, and wild buffalo. Look out for the special Information Packs and Museum stops, too. During your journey all the facts you will learn are true, and the stops on our journey are real places that you could visit with your family.

On each double-page you will follow a different section of the journey and there is a map so that you can follow the route and see where the numbered stops are. After reading the introduction to each section, follow the stops in order until you reach the end of the page, when you will be whisked off to the next stage of the journey.

A fascinating adventure is waiting for you, so turn the page and enjoy your *Journey through North America*.

CONTENTS

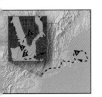
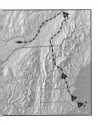

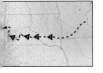

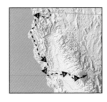

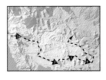
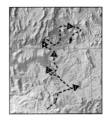

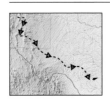

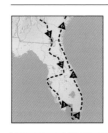

Key

 route

 place visited

river

 country border

 state border

NEW YORK CITY

We begin our journey in the exciting city of New York, on the east coast of North America. Each year 7 million visitors from around the world come to see its many sites. There are so many fascinating buildings, art galleries, theatres, restaurants, and department stores in New York that it is difficult to decide what to do.

Our first stop is Manhattan, the borough (area) of New York City where most of the sites are located. In lower Manhattan we take a walk down Wall Street, one of the world's most important banking centres. Nearby, we board a ferry to Liberty Island, where America's best-known statue stands, and then continue on to Ellis Island. This is where the grandparents and great-grandparents of half of America's population first arrived from Europe. Finally, we leave the city and drive to Cape Cod, Massachusetts, to see some whales.

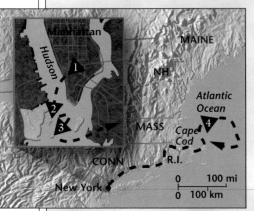

▼ Manhattan

Many people in Manhattan work in the banking, advertising, entertainment, and fashion industries. Here on Wall Street, stocks and shares of companies are bought and sold at the New York Stock Exchange. The ups and downs of these financial 'markets' influence economies all over the world. As you walk along the streets, be sure to look upwards at the giant skyscrapers for which the city is famous. Not far from Wall Street are the twin towers of the World Trade Center, which stretch 110 stories into the sky.

Manhattan is actually an island, lying between the Hudson and East rivers. There are views across the Hudson River as we walk towards Battery Park at the southern tip of the island. From here we will take a ferry to our next stop.

◄ Liberty Island

Stepping off the ferry you may be amazed by the size of the Statue of Liberty. From its base it stands 72 metres high and weighs 225 tons. The nose alone is 138 centimetres long! The French built the Statue as a gift to America. In 1884 it was shipped over in several pieces and then rebuilt on the island. Inside the statue there are 154 steps from the base up to Liberty's crown. From the crown you can see far into the distance. For European immigrants coming to America by ship, the Statue of Liberty with its lit torch must have been a magnificent sight.

3 Ellis Island

Between 1892 and 1954, twelve million immigrants from around the world came to live in America. Ellis Island was their first stop. You can watch films in the museum which tell of families who escaped persecution in their homeland by coming here. Some were so poor and ill that they died on their journey over. But many found work in America and were successful.

4 Whale-watching

We've now left the crowds of New York City. Here, off the coast of Cape Cod in Massachusetts, we get a good look at some humpback whales swimming along Stellwagon Bank. Whales sometimes come so close to the boat that you can feel the spray of water that shoots out from the blowhole on their head. Whales eat millions of microscopic sea creatures called plankton. It seems strange that an animal so big would want to eat something so small. Seals and dolphins also live nearby, but they prefer eating fish.

From Cape Cod we set off through New England.

NEW ENGLAND

Connecticut, Maine, Massachusetts, Vermont, and New Hampshire are the northeastern states that make up the region of New England. The landscape is varied, with forests, mountains, farmland, marshes, and miles of rugged coastline.

First we follow the coast road to Plimoth Plantation in Massachusetts where English Pilgrims first came to live in 1620. We see a full-size reproduction of the ship they bravely sailed in and look at how Pilgrims lived and dressed. Next we head northwest to the historic city of Boston to learn about some important events that led to the American Revolutionary War. In the city we visit the site of an 18th-century battleground. A long car journey takes us inland from Boston, and through the countryside to enjoy the rich colours of a real New England fall. Following this we continue north and cross the border into Canada. We take a rest in a grand hotel in the old, French-speaking city of Quebec.

◀ 2 Boston

In 1773 the people of Boston protested against British taxes on their tea by dumping crates of tea into the harbour. This angered Britain, and the two countries were soon at war. A battle was fought in Boston at Bunker Hill in 1775. Britain won it but with heavy losses. In Boston today local people are acting out the battle.

▲ 1 Plimoth Plantation

The Pilgrims were the first immigrants to settle in New England. *Mayflower II* is a copy of the ship which brought them here in 1620. Nearby, on Plimoth Plantation, you can see how the Pilgrims of the 17th century dressed and lived.

▼ New England

We visit New England in the fall (autumn), when it is a special treat to see. The cold nights cause the leaves of sugar maple trees to turn beautiful shades of yellow, orange, and red. Every February, sap is collected from these trees and boiled down into delicious maple syrup. Look out for pumpkins, too, as they are harvested and sold in local markets during the fall. Native Americans taught the Pilgrims how to grow pumpkins, which became very important as they could be stored during the cold winter months when few crops grew successfully. The Pilgrims were used to warmer winters so many of the vegetable crops they first tried to grow failed. Today, people still eat pumpkins, but they also use them for making scarecrows and lanterns at Halloween.

INFORMATION PACK

Many of the Pilgrims who arrived on the *Mayflower* belonged to a religious group called the Puritans. They left England because they were unhappy with the Anglican Church and felt they were unfairly treated. The Puritans had strict rules about the way they dressed and worshipped. They lived in simple homes and wore plain, dark clothes. Their children were taught to read the Bible every day.

▲ Le Chateau Frontenac

In Quebec we stay at Le Chateau Frontenac – a grand, 19th-century hotel, overlooking the St Lawrence river. The French settled in Quebec in the 17th century. Everyone here still speaks French and no signposts are in English. Quebec is the only walled city in North America.

We drive through Montreal on our way to the province of Ontario.

THE NIAGARA FALLS

The Niagara river forms part of the border between the United States and Canada, and both countries look after their section of the Niagara Falls. The Horseshoe Falls in Canada measure 51 metres high and 792 metres wide. The American Falls in New York State measure 54 metres high and 305 metres wide. Some of the gushing water is diverted to make electricity at nearby power plants.

We fly over the Falls later, but our first stop in Ontario is in the Algonquin Provincial Park. We set up camp here and try to find our way through the wilderness of lakes and forests. Then it's back to civilization as we visit Canada's largest city, Toronto, for a look at the world's tallest free-standing structure. After Niagara Falls, we head for the industrial city of Detroit to look at the works of famous inventors.

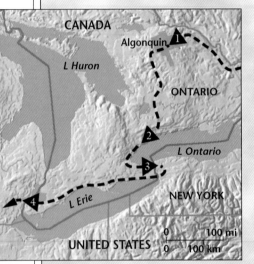

CANADA
Algonquin 1
L Huron
ONTARIO
2
L Ontario
3
NEW YORK
4 L Erie
UNITED STATES
0   100 mi
0   100 km

▼ 1 Algonquin Provincial Park

Our campsite by Timberwolf Lake in Algonquin Park is wonderfully peaceful. You may catch a glimpse of a bull moose wading through the water, feeding on its favourite food – water plants. The park has a hundred lakes and only one road, so when we leave the campsite in the morning we have to read our map carefully and get back before dark.

◄ 2 Toronto

Toronto, on the northwest shore of Lake Ontario, is Canada's largest city. Here, we visit the world's tallest free-standing structure, the Canadian National (CN) Tower. Built as a radio and television transmitter, it stands 533 metres high. We take the lift to the observation deck at the top for some fantastic views.

3 Niagara Falls

We board a plane to see the splendour of the Niagara Falls from above. It is also possible to take a boat trip along the Niagara river to view the Falls as they come crashing down. There are guided tours through the rocky tunnels behind the Falls, where the water flows so thick and fast it blocks out the daylight. The rocky ledge over which the water cascades was formed over 400 million years ago. Very few particles of the hard rock are washed away as the water cascades over the edge, which is why the Falls look so clear. Imagine how it looked when, during a cold spring in 1848, the water upstream froze and the Niagara Falls became nothing more than a tiny trickle!

 MUSEUM STOP

4 Henry Ford Museum

In Detroit's Ford Museum you can see many old cars, including this 1909 Ford Model T, the first car to be mass-produced. Henry Ford founded the Ford Motor Company in 1903. You can also see many other items that changed peoples' lives. There is the lab where Edison invented the light bulb, and the bicycle shop where the Wright brothers built their first plane!

INFORMATION PACK

Detroit is famous for music as well as cars. In 1959 the record company Tamla Motown was founded by Berry Gordy in a small house on Grand Boulevard in Detroit. Gordy discovered many black pop stars, such as Diana Ross and the Supremes (below), Stevie Wonder, and Michael Jackson, who brought the 'Motown Sound' to the pop-charts of the 1960s.

We ride on Detroit's People Mover train before exploring the Great Lakes.

THE GREAT LAKES

Lakes Huron, Ontario, Erie, Michigan, and Superior are the largest group of freshwater lakes in the world. Long ago they were used by explorers to get around the Northwest Territory (Indiana, Ohio, Illinois, Michigan, Wisconsin, and Minnesota). Today, canals connect the lakes, and large ships can travel from them to any port in the world.

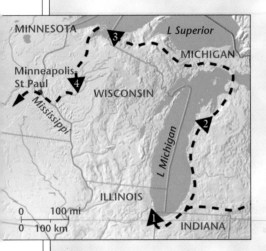

Our first stop is Chicago, Illinois, on the shore of Lake Michigan. It is America's third-largest city and the home of the Chicago Bulls basketball team. Our next stop, Traverse City, Michigan, is an important fruit-growing region of the Great Lakes. From there, we drive north to Lake Superior and take a boat trip around the Apostle Islands before visiting a museum to learn about the lives of some early explorers.

Next we take a cycle ride past miles of orchards and vineyards. The warm air that blows over from Lake Michigan raises the air temperatures just enough to make this part of Michigan an excellent fruit-producing region. Here, thousands of hectares of cherry trees are grown and the area is known to many Americans as the 'Cherry Capital of the World'. Every July the residents of Traverse City hold a cherry festival to celebrate their harvest. There are parades, fireworks, and bands playing in the streets. If you get hungry, there are ice-creams, cakes, and drinks all made with freshly-picked cherries.

◀ Chicago

At tonight's basketball game in the United Center, the Chicago Bulls are playing the Detroit Pistons. Michael Jordan, now retired, will always be remembered as one of the Bulls' best players. Jordan was voted the World's Greatest Athlete in a USA poll.

The people of Chicago love their sports teams, including the Blackhawks (ice-hockey), the Bears (American football), and the Cubs and White Sox (baseball).

③ Apostle Islands

Now we travel by motorboat to Madeline Island, one of the 22 Apostle Islands on Lake Superior. As we glide along, we pass rose-coloured cliffs with caves and hollows carved by the icy waters. The forests on the islands are quite new. The original forests were destroyed over time by loggers and forest fires. But in 1970 the islands became a conservation area and new forests have been developed. If we are lucky, and not too noisy, we may see some black bears. Black bears are omnivorous. This means they will eat almost anything, including fish, berries, and wild birds' eggs. An adult bear can eat up to 40 kilograms of food each day!

 MUSEUM STOP

④ Chippewa Valley Museum

Here we learn about the history of the Chippewa tribe of Native Americans who lived in this area. Like much of Wisconsin, the area was once thickly forested and in the 1880s people came from Germany and Scandinavia to work in the timber camps. We see a sturdy Scandinavian-style log cabin, built to keep out the wind. By the end of the 19th century much of the Chippewa land had been sold to the timber companies. The Chippewa worked in logging too, but were not allowed to hunt, fish, or trap as they had done before. This caused great hardship. But by 1979, laws had been passed giving them back their rights.

INFORMATION PACK

A quarter of a million years ago, thick sheets of ice, called glaciers, moved slowly south across what is now called the Great Lakes region. The glaciers weighed thousands of tonnes and were several kilometres thick. As they moved, they pushed rocks along, which tore deep holes into the ground. This and the great weight and movement of the melting glaciers caused layers of the earth to slowly sink, creating lake beds. As the glaciers melted, the vast amounts of water did not drain away and the Great Lakes and surrounding wetlands were formed.

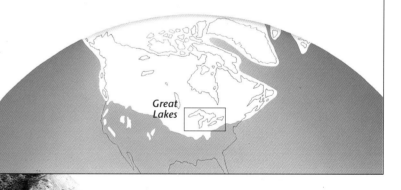

Great Lakes

At Minneapolis-St Paul we cross the Mississippi River.

THE BADLANDS

The region of the Great Plains known as the Badlands was a saltwater sea millions of years ago. Over time the climate changed and the water began to dry up. Few plants grew in the thin soil and the soft rock underneath became exposed to the harsh weather. Over a million years, wind and rain wore away the different layers of mud and sandstone, carving strange shapes into the earth.

Outside the Badlands are huge stretches of farmland. There are National Parks, too, where coyote, bighorn sheep, and deer are free to roam. While in the Buffalo National Grassland we see some prairie dogs, which make their homes underground. Then we drive through the Badlands National Park to look at some amazing rock formations. In the Black Hills National Forest, we see how dynamite has turned a mountain into a monument. Finally, we head west towards Devil's Tower, an ancient volcano which is now a huge stone stump.

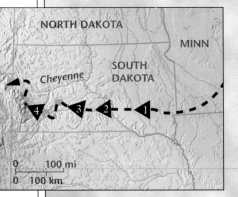

NORTH DAKOTA
MINN
SOUTH DAKOTA
Cheyenne
4 3 2 1
0   100 mi
0 100 km

2 Buffalo National Grassland

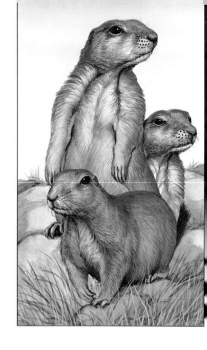

Thousands of prairie dogs live in the grasslands. Although they are called dogs they are actually small burrowing rodents which belong to the squirrel family. They live more than a metre underground in groups called coteries. The system of tunnels they dig may cover several kilometres. During the day prairie dogs feed on grass and seeds. If they smell danger, they bark loudly to each other and run back into their tunnels.

1 Wheatfields

As we travel across the Great Plains we see vast areas of farmland. Wild grasses once covered the Great Plains, but since the 1870s farming began to take over. Instead of wild grasses, cereal crops such as wheat cover large areas. The United States is now the world's largest exporter of wheat. We stop for a while and watch a man operate a combine harvester – he has probably been hired by local farmers to cut thousands of hectares of wheat.

⑶ Badlands

We are lucky to be travelling in an air-conditioned motorhome – we can see heatwaves rising from the ground (temperatures range from –51 to 49 °C). The oddly shaped, rainbow-coloured rocks are bone dry and very little grows in the thin soil. Somehow, mammals like prairie dogs, mule deer, and wild sheep find enough food to keep healthy but they have to beware of hungry coyotes (prairie wolves), like the ones we can see on the hilltop.

⑷ Mt Rushmore

Here in the Black Hills the faces of four American presidents – George Washington, Thomas Jefferson, Theodore Roosevelt, and Abraham Lincoln – are carved into the cliff of Mt Rushmore. It took the sculptor and a team of engineers fourteen years (from 1927 until 1941) to complete the project. They drilled, carved, and blasted into the granite rock with dynamite. Each head measures about 18 metres from top to bottom.

INFORMATION PACK

Sitting Bull was leader of the Sioux, a tribe of Native Americans who lived in the Great Plains. The Sioux were skilled warriors who fought the US government over land rights. Having defeated General Custer's army in 1876, Sitting Bull fled to Canada. He returned in 1881 and was imprisoned for two years.

On our way to Mammoth Springs, we pass Devil's Tower. ▶

THE HOT SPRINGS

This part of our journey takes us into an area of Wyoming that is well known for its geothermal springs. These appear as boiling mud pools, cascading falls, and exploding geysers that bubble up from deep within the earth, where the water is heated by hot rocks. We visit some of these natural wonders in America's oldest and best known National Park, Yellowstone.

Our first stop is the Little Bighorn museum. Here, we learn why the US government wanted

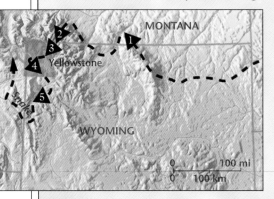

to force Native Americans off the Great Plains and we visit the site of the famous battle that was fought between the US army and the Sioux and Cheyenne tribes. Next, we visit Mammoth Hot Springs and Old Faithful in Yellowstone Park. Then we put on our life-jackets and take a dingy down Snake River to view the breathtaking scenery of the Grand Teton mountain range.

⬛ MUSEUM STOP

▶ 1 Little Bighorn

It took the US government many years to force the Native Americans off the Great Plains and onto reservations. The government hoped to find gold and other minerals in the region, and to build railroads and farms there. However, the Sioux and Cheyenne tribes had always lived and hunted over a wide area of land, and they fought many battles against the US army to defend their rights. The most famous battle took place in 1876, when General George Custer (right) and his men were defeated by Sioux and Cheyenne warriors.

▼ 2 Yellowstone National Park

At the Mammoth Hot Springs, in the northern part of Yellowstone Park, water boils up from deep inside the earth. It spills noisily over terraces of limestone rock, depositing calcium as it goes. Algae and bacteria (simple forms of plant and animal life) grow in the pools of warm water that collect in the terraces. These give the terraces their beautiful colours, and their unpleasant smells! When the explorer John Colter first arrived here in 1807, no one believed his reports of what he had seen. The US government eventually sent its own explorers to the area. They were so amazed by the landscape, hot springs, and wildlife, that in 1872 they made Yellowstone America's first National Park.

Yellowstone covers 900,000 hectares and within it is one of America's largest wildlife sanctuaries. You can camp and hike in Yellowstone for days and always find something new. Make sure you bring your binoculars along – you may be able to spot the United States' national bird, the bald eagle. In the quieter areas of the park you may see elk, grizzly bear, and bison, and numerous fish and birds of prey. But take care to lock your food away from hungry bears!

▶ 3 Old Faithful Geyser

Geysers are natural springs of water which heat up to boiling point deep inside the earth, where there is volcanic activity. Old Faithful is the most popular of the 200 active geysers in Yellowstone Park. However, you have to wait for it to perform. At first water just bubbles around the rim of the hole. Suddenly a huge fountain shoots up, with about 38,000 litres of water reaching 60 metres into the air. It is a spectacular site but you must take care to stand well back to avoid being scalded. Trails take us to other geysers in the area too. They have all been given names, too, such as Beehive, Giant, and Daisy.

▼ 4 Bison

Among the many kinds of mammals to be seen in Yellowstone are bison, also known as buffalo. Once there were millions of bison roaming the Great Plains but in the 19th century they were hunted for their skins until there were almost no bison left. They now live protected in national parks.

▲ 5 Snake River

From Yellowstone we make our way south to Grand Teton National Park. The jagged and snow-covered mountains rise up sharply around gentle valleys and meadows. There are no roads crossing through the mountains, but we can explore the foot-hills and walk near the lakes and pools which were created here thousands of years ago by melting glaciers. We need sturdy life jackets as we raft along Snake River to get a good view of the mountains. Snake River winds its way through four north-western states (Wyoming, Idaho, Oregon, and Washington).

We drive north through Idaho, with the Teton mountains behind us.

THE PLAINS INDIANS

The Sioux, Cheyenne, Blackfoot, and Crow are the major tribes of Native Americans who live on the Great Plains. During the 1800s, they used their excellent horseriding skills to hunt the enormous herds of bison that roamed the American West. The Plains Indians did not stay in one area or farm land as the white settlers did; instead they lived and hunted over many miles.

We begin our trip in Bozeman, Montana. Here, we go to a rodeo to see cowboys show off their riding 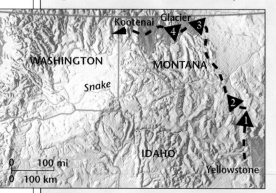 and roping skills. Next, in Helena, the state capital, we watch a traditional Native American pow-wow. From there, we take a hike along the cool, alpine meadows of Glacier National Park which gets its name from the deep valleys that were carved out by glaciers thousands of years ago. Further west, we camp deep in the woods of Kootenai National Forest and learn about the kinds of wild food we can gather for our dinner.

1 Bozeman

Rodeo used to be a way of rounding up cattle but today it is a professional sport. This rodeo rider is trying to stay on a wild horse for 10 seconds without being thrown off. Rodeos have many dangerous events and the cowboys can get badly injured. But those who do well can earn a lot of prize money.

2 Helena

A pow-wow is a Native American gathering where people from a particular tribe dress in traditional costume and dance, sing, and say prayers in their native language. It may be part of a religious ceremony or simply a way of welcoming a new family into a community. The pow-wow we are visiting is for students who have worked hard at school all year and received good grades. Their families will be presented with useful gifts such as tools and blankets. There are also some dance contests. People of all ages join in, from tiny children to grandparents. They spend a long time preparing their clothes. Every detail, from head to toe, must be just right because their costumes are judged, too.

3 Glacier National Park

We are high up in the mountains where the air is cold and fresh. There are streams, wildflower meadows, forests, and fish-filled lakes. You may spot grizzly bears and mountain lions hunting their prey near the lakes. The mountain goats you can see have special hooves that help them to run and climb through ice and snow.

INFORMATION PACK

Meriwether Lewis and William Clark first explored the Northwest Territory in 1804. They set off from Missouri and travelled 12,000 kilometres to the Pacific coast. They met many Native Americans who helped them find their way. Lewis and Clark made maps of the area and kept notes of the natural resources. As the area was not owned by other Europeans, the US government felt free to include it as part of the developing United States. As a result, many white settlers came to live in the West.

4 Kootenai National Forest

In this National Forest we climb up a lookout tower and are lucky enough to see an eagle's nest. Our campsite is surrounded by streams and a lake, and the weather is damp. These are ideal conditions for mosquitoes to breed, so we must use insect repellent to avoid being bitten. It is hard to imagine that there are forest fires here each year. Sometimes started by lightning, forest fires are difficult to control. Occasionally they are left to burn, as the fires clear away dead wood and make space for younger trees to grow.

Later, we search for huckleberries. They grow by the edge of the forest and taste delicious cooked with pancakes.

Next, we board an Amtrak train and head for Washington State.

THE RAINFOREST

On this stage of our journey, we visit the only temperate rainforest in continental USA. Rainforests are important habitats for plants and animals. They are important in other ways, too. Each year, rare rainforest plants are found to have chemicals in them which can be turned into useful medicines. Research is being done on these plants in the hope that they may one day be used for the treatment of cancer.

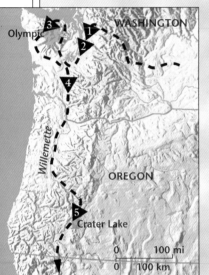

We begin this section of our journey in Seattle at the site of the 1962 World's Fair before taking a tour around the city's Museum of Flight. Next, we drive up to Olympic National Park. Then, in contrast to the park's lush green rainforest, we visit the scarred landscape around Mt St Helens, which erupted in 1980. After a break, we go to Crater Lake National Park and see how another, more destructive volcano has become a haven for wildlife and tourists.

 MUSEUM STOP

The Museum of Flight

The Boeing corporation was founded near Seattle in 1916 and aircraft manufacturing is one of Seattle's biggest industries. So it comes as no surprise that the Museum of Flight is the city's largest museum. Here in the Great Gallery, there are twenty full-sized aircraft, many of them suspended from the ceiling. The large aircraft on the ground is the Blackbird Spyplane that could fly at three times the speed of sound.

Seattle

Seattle is a big, modern city. Many people living here work for companies that produce aircraft or computer software. The city has trendy cafes and interesting museums, tall glass skyscrapers, and a good public transport system. We take the monorail to the Seattle Center, a complex built for the 1962 World's Fair, which was held in Seattle. The Space Needle was meant to look like a building designed in the 21st century. For a better look at the city, we take the glass lift up to the Needle's observation deck. If it's not fully booked, we can have a meal in the restaurant at the top!

Olympic National Park

The Olympic National Park's weather is mild but very, very wet. It receives more rainfall than anywhere else in continental USA. The Olympic mountains trap much of the moisture in the lower forests and the rain and rich soil encourage lush plant growth. Giant fir trees block out the sun and 300 species of shade-loving plants, like ferns and mosses, grow thick and green. There are plenty of unusual mushrooms growing on damp forest logs and big, yellow slugs which feed on rotting vegetation. Larger wildlife in the park include the shy, Roosevelt elk.

4 Mt St Helens

In May 1980, Mt St Helens erupted in Washington State, killing 57 people and over a million wild animals. The timber industry was ruined as thousands of hectares of forest were burnt and buried under thick volcanic ash. The finer particles of ash stayed high in the atmosphere blocking out some of the sunlight. These clouds affected the weather across most of America that summer. But now the forest is slowly coming back to life.

INFORMATION PACK

In the mid-1800s, thousands of settlers travelled west along the Oregon Trail to purchase land and build homes. They covered huge distances of open country, often herding livestock with them. The journey, which took six months, began in Independence, Missouri and ended in the Willamette Valley of Oregon – a distance of about 3,200 kilometres.

5 Crater Lake National Park

Mt St Helens' eruption was tiny compared with Mt Mazama's explosion 7,000 years ago. The blast was so powerful it left a huge crater in its place. Slowly, melting snow and rain filled the crater and a beautiful, clear lake was created. Today the area is a haven for wildlife, such as this mountain lion.

A Greyhound bus takes us through forests into California.

21

THE GOLDEN GATE BRIDGE

San Francisco is a leading financial and international trade centre for the western USA. Its population of nearly 750,000 is multi-racial – there are people from many ethnic backgrounds including Chinese, Japanese, Hispanic, and African American. The city is bordered by the Pacific Ocean on the west and San Francisco Bay on the east. Its famous landmark, the Golden Gate Bridge, spans the opening to the city's deep-water harbour.

We begin our journey across California by driving through a tree! Then we take the wine train through Napa Valley, famous for its vineyards. From there we tour San Francisco and drive across the Golden Gate Bridge. We also learn about the earthquakes that threaten the area. Next, we go to an old mining town and learn how to pan for gold. Finally, we take a trip to a National Park to admire the scenery.

▶ Redwood National Park

In the Redwood National Park we see some of the world's tallest trees. Redwoods can measure more than 90 metres tall, and some are thought to be over 3,500 years of age! The National Park forest in which they grow is dense and dark and smells strongly of pine needles. Continuing south to the town of Leggett, we drive through the trunk of a redwood! A tunnel has been carved so that cars can drive through rather than around the giant tree.

▼ Napa Valley

The Napa Valley is warm and sunny and ideal for growing wine grapes. Thousands of hectares of vineyards are planted and grape juice is processed and wine bottled on nearby estates.

The weather here is often foggy, but we are lucky to arrive on a day when the fog is beginning to clear. The view across the Bay is dazzling. The Golden Gate Bridge is visible from almost every high spot in hilly San Francisco. Built in 1937, its soaring, 227-metre-high towers make driving across it a real thrill. The bridge is 1,280 metres long. It is a suspension bridge, with the roadway suspended from cables, strung between the two towers. In 1987, a quarter of a million people gathered on the bridge at sunrise to celebrate its fiftieth anniversary. It was a windy day and the weight of so many people made the bridge buckle, but it did not break.

San Franciscans are used to living dangerously since their city is built on the San Andreas fault line (see the Information Pack). The city was devastated by an earthquake in 1906 and there was another major quake in 1989.

INFORMATION PACK

The Earth's crust is made up of plates. At the San Andreas fault line, which stretches over 1,000 kilometres through the state of California, two plates are sliding past each other. As they rub together they release energy, sometimes causing earthquakes. San Francisco lies on the fault line and has experienced several devastating earthquakes. The force of a quake is measured on the Richter scale, which ranges from 1 (minor quakes) to 8 (massive earth-shaking quakes).

🏛 MUSEUM STOP

4 Columbia State Park

In the 1850s, a group of miners discovered an area of land rich in gold-bearing rock. They set up camp and extracted the gold using high-pressure jets of water. The small camp soon became crowded as thousands of miners, hoping to get rich, moved there. By the 1860s, much of the gold was gone and the miners left. The town has been kept as a living museum of that time. You can even look for gold yourself.

Yosemite National Park **5** ▶

North America's highest waterfall is here in Yosemite. It tumbles down 740 metres. The park is surrounded by sheer granite cliffs. These popular cliffs attract many rock climbers, although in the summer the rockface can heat up to 37 °C.

We drive past Yosemite's Cathedral Spires on our way south.

THE VALLEY OF DEATH

As its name suggests, Death Valley in California gets dangerously hot – hotter than anywhere else on Earth. Temperatures of 45°C are not uncommon in the summer. The ground can heat up to boiling point (100°C). Death Valley is surrounded by weather-worn canyons and mineral-rich rocks and hills. From Dante's View in the Black Mountains, you can see Mt Whitney and Badwater – the highest and lowest points in continental USA.

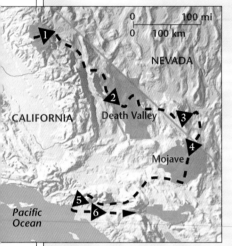

First we drive to Mono Lake, which is shrinking as the demand for water increases in California. Then we head into Death Valley, stocked up with lots of drinks and sunscreen to keep us alive and well. We cool off in Las Vegas before exploring the high desert of Mojave. Then we head for Malibu Beach, famous for its surfing. Finally, we visit Beverly Hills, home to many of the rich and famous.

▶ Mono Lake

The tufa lumps may look like strange sandcastles, but they are actually calcium deposits brought up from underground springs. The lumps used to lie deep in the mineral-rich water of Mono Lake, but have been exposed as the water table has gone down. The water level has changed dramatically over the last fifty years because of the increased demand for water from surrounding cities. The area is an important stopover point for migratory birds such as geese, swans, and ducks. Mono Lake's shores provide nesting sites for many California gulls, too.

▼ Death Valley

We have just driven into Death Valley. The sun is scorching hot and there is very little shade. They say you can fry eggs on the ground. Violent sandstorms and dust whirlwinds, sometimes lasting several hours, blow across the valley. Fortunately we have brought plenty of drinking water with us so that we don't become dehydrated. Although nothing seems to be growing here now, after the spring rains thousands of tiny wild-flower seeds, which have lain still in the soil for months, will grow and their blossoms will fill the desert with colour.

We hired a classic American car for this part of the journey – but we can take it no further here. Instead, if we are careful about the heat, we will perhaps take a short walk across Death Valley to see what a beautiful place it can be.

3 Las Vegas

Though not far from Death Valley, Las Vegas seems a world away. Hotels and gambling casinos line the streets, and neon lights flash from every wall. Most buildings in Las Vegas have a theme. The Excalibur Hotel has a legendary theme and is designed to look like King Arthur's castle. Thank goodness the beds are modern and comfortable!

4 Mojave Desert

It is very quiet in the Mojave Desert and it gets quite cool at night. When we arrive it has recently rained and the desert is in bloom. Cold-blooded animals such as this rare desert tortoise need to warm themselves in the sun before they can go off in search of food.

5 Malibu

Surfing is a good way to keep cool in summer, but it takes lots of practice. You need to be a strong swimmer and have good balance. All along the Pacific Coast Highway there are surf shops selling surf equipment. But not everyone is here to surf. Some people come to Malibu hoping to see movie stars who own beach houses near the ocean.

6 Witches' House

Beverly Hills is a wealthy suburb of Los Angeles. Many movie stars live here in big mansions. This house is very different to most in Beverly Hills. It was built in the 1920s as a movie set before it was rebuilt here.

We leave Los Angeles in style and drive past Hollywood.

HOLLYWOOD

THE WILD WEST

In the 1800s, large areas of the west in America were undeveloped. Many easterners began to move there because land was cheap and they heard that there was money to be made from gold and silver mining. The Arizona territory was particularly attractive to prospectors and they moved there in great numbers. Towns were built in a hurry but there were few sheriffs to keep law and order.

As we travel towards Arizona our route passes some amazing plants. The Joshua tree is unusual because it can grow in conditions that would kill most plant life. The cactus is another hardy plant, and at the Organpipe Cactus National Monument we see how it survives with so little rain. We learn more about desert wildlife at the Sonora desert museum before visiting the historical town of Tombstone, just in time to see a cowboy shoot-out from the Wild West.

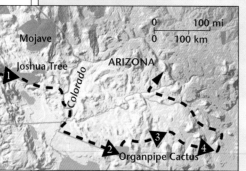

◀ Joshua Tree National Park

These unusual trees were named after the Biblical prophet Joshua. They may look rather odd and misshapen but they have done well to grow in such a harsh environment. The desert is not just hot and dry – there are sometimes flash floods and high winds. The floods wash away the thin soil, making it difficult for plant roots to anchor themselves into the rocky cliffs. Climbers and hikers in the park have to take care to read their maps and keep to marked trails. There are many abandoned goldmines here and it would be all too easy to fall down an unused mine-shaft!

◀ Organpipe Cactus National Monument

There can be a long wait for rain in the desert. Cactus roots grow close to the surface of the soil so that any rain that falls will be quickly absorbed. Water is stored in the flesh of the cactus and the plant lives off this until the next rains come.

 MUSEUM STOP

3 Sonora Desert Museum

A Gila monster is a large lizard, native to the American southwest. It hunts at night and feeds on small mammals and reptiles. If bothered, it can give you a nasty bite. In the wild, female Gila monsters lay their eggs in sand and then abandon them. After about a month the eggs hatch and the babies have to look after themselves. At the museum's wildlife centre we see many other desert animals, too, such as the Mexican wolf and wild turkey. Some were found injured and will be set free when

4 Tombstone

Many people were lured to western mining towns hoping to get rich. As there were few police to enforce the law, criminals went too. In 1879 the Earp brothers came to live in Tombstone. They were all skilled gunmen and two were part-time policemen. Wyatt Earp became a US Marshal. He was keen to rid the town of criminals, but soon made enemies with known cattle thieves, the Clanton and the McLaury brothers. Wyatt heard rumours that the thieves hoped to run him and his brothers out of Tombstone, but the Earps were determined it would be the other way round. Like many disputes in the Wild West, it ended in a terrible shoot-out. One Clanton and both McLaury brothers were killed. The Marshal and his brothers were accused of murder but, as there were no witnesses willing to come forward, the charges against them were dropped. Today, Tombstone is a historical site and each year you can watch actors re-playing the shoot-out near the OK Corral. The Earps are dressed in black.

On our way to the Grand Canyon we pass the Superstition mountains.

THE GRAND CANYON

Canyons are deep-sided ravines which form gradually as water cuts through soft rock. The Grand Canyon is over 430 kilometres long, 2 kilometres deep and, in some spots, over 20 kilometres wide. At the bottom flows the Colorado River. It is a popular place to go whitewater rafting, camping, and hiking. When it became a National Park in 1919, the Grand Canyon had just over 44,000 visitors a year. Today, nearly 5 million visitors arrive each year.

Before we visit the Grand Canyon, our journey takes us to the Pertified Forest. Here we see the remains of ancient fossilized trees, unearthed by erosion. Further west we take an exciting helicopter ride over the Grand Canyon and then travel on to Lake Powell, a huge artificial lake. From there we visit Bryce Canyon to look at some strange stone formations before heading east to a bizarre landscape of over 2,000 stone arches.

From our helicopter, we can see the Colorado River winding its way along the bottom of the canyon. At certain times of the day, the sun highlights the different layers of rock that form the walls on either side of the river. Millions of tourists camp along the rim of the canyon and many take mule rides down steep trails to the water. 'River running' (rafting) is an exciting way to explore the river. But it is very important to remember that the Grand Canyon is a desert wilderness. The demand for water from tourists puts a strain on the park's resources and the pollution from so many cars spoils the air quality. Environmentalists are trying to find ways of letting people enjoy this great park without damaging nature.

▲ 1 The Petrified Forest

These fossilized logs date back to the Triassic period, 225 million years ago. Many dinosaurs roamed the earth at about this time, and the logs were then large conifer trees growing quite far away from here. The trees were washed into the area by a flood and buried under mud and volcanic ash. Over time, mineral deposits from floodwater seeped into the cells of the trees and turned what was left of them into stone.

3 Lake Powell

This is America's second largest artificial lake. Environmentalists fought against the plans to build a dam and flood the unspoiled wilderness of Glen Canyon. But many others believed that a large body of water was needed if people were to develop land for farming, housing and tourism. It now attracts 3.5 million visitors a year.

4 Bryce Canyon

While standing beside some tall sandstone formations, a guide tells us that it is the wind and rain that has carved the rocks into these strange shapes. The formations are called 'hoodoos'. Some people think hoodoos look like stone soldiers, tree trunks, or even wild animals.

5 Arches National Park

Here we take a ride on mountain bikes to see a few of the natural arches in the park. Like the hoodoos, they are sandstone formations worn away by the weather.

Next we drive south, towards Monument Valley.

29

THE RED ROCK TOWERS

Many artists are attracted to Monument Valley. They congregate here to sketch or paint the dramatic landscape of towering red and gold rocks. Every evening at sunset, the Mittens, a pair of sandstone towers measuring over 500 metres high, seem to glow a fiery red. Several famous movies have also been filmed here, including *Back to the Future III*, so the landscape of Monument Valley is well-known to many.

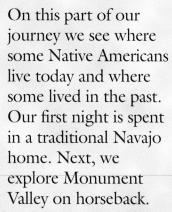

On this part of our journey we see where some Native Americans live today and where some lived in the past. Our first night is spent in a traditional Navajo home. Next, we explore Monument Valley on horseback. From there we cross the border into Colorado to visit the site of an early Native American settlement. Further south we visit Taos Pueblo to see a different kind of Native American house. Finally, we explore the busy city of Albuquerque.

Navajo Reservation

We stop off for the night at a Navajo reservation, before exploring Monument Valley. We sleep in a traditional hogan home. Not all Native Americans lived in tee-pees. The Navajo farmed their land and needed more permanent housing. These homes are made with wooden poles and are covered with earth and rocks – they are very sturdy. Hogan homes keep cool during the intense daytime heat and are warm and cosy at night.

Monument Valley

We learn from our guide that a plateau is a raised area of land which is very flat on top. A mesa is smaller and more like an island of flat-topped rock. The thin, hard rock towers sticking up in the distance are called buttes. They have been worn narrow by the wind and sharp sand. Monument Valley is on Navajo reservation land. The Navajo are skilled farmers. They graze sheep and grow crops with very little water. Maize is grown near the sides of canyons so that any rain that falls runs straight onto the crops. The Navajos have their own banks, schools, and community centres. We are made to feel very welcome on the reservation, but must remember to respect their rules. For example, it is polite to ask permission before taking photographs.

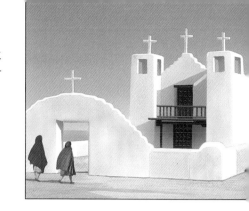

3 ◀ Mesa Verde National Park

The Anasazi were ancestors of many southwest Native American tribes. They lived in this area between AD 500 and the 13th century and were among the earliest tribes to settle and farm the land. They grew maize and reared livestock for food and clothing. Over the years, they learned to build sturdy homes in the rocky alcoves of mountains. Here at Mesa Verde National Park we see the ruins of their dwellings.

4 ▲ Taos Pueblo

Pueblo is Spanish for 'village'. The buildings in Taos are made from adobe, a sun-baked mud, covered in white to reflect the desert heat. Spanish missionaries built adobe churches and taught Native Americans to be Christian.

5 ▲ Albuquerque

Albuquerque (pronounced 'Alba-ker-key') was settled by the Spanish in the 18th century and is now New Mexico's biggest city. At the Pueblo Cultural Center we see some traditional Native American jewellery, made of silver and turquoise, a precious stone. At the New Mexico Museum of Natural History, we watch a simulated (pretend) volcanic eruption and get to touch some dinosaur bones and fossils. We end the day with a hot and spicy meal at a Mexican restaurant. Outside, an important ingredient in our meal is being sold – hot chilli peppers.

On the way to the Carlsbad Caverns, we pass the Rio Grande.

31

THE CARLSBAD CAVERNS

Below the Guadaloupe mountains of New Mexico we visit one of the largest cave systems in the world and home to thousands of bats. Native Americans knew of the caves but did not explore them because the entrances were so steep. Miners at the turn of the century dug out 'guano' (bat droppings), a valuable fertilizer, from inside the cave entrances. The more they dug, the deeper inside the caves they went.

As we head towards the southern part of New Mexico, we find ourselves sharing the road with a bird! We then take a walk through powdery white sand dunes before descending deep inside the Carlsbad Caverns for a good look at what those early miners found. Next, we head east into Texas and visit a cattle ranch. Finally, we see the Alamo, a site that many Texans are proud of.

▶ Roadrunner

The roadrunner is a member of the cuckoo family. It is also the New Mexico state bird. Although it can fly, the roadrunner prefers to walk along the desert floor (and often the roads) in search of small reptiles. If disturbed, it can run at speeds of up to 25 kilometres an hour.

❷ White Sands

The 'sand' here is really gypsum, a chalky rock used in making cement. Rain dissolves gypsum from nearby mountains. When it dries, winds blow the powdered rock into huge white dunes.

❸ Carlsbad Caverns

The strange icicle-shaped rocks are called stalactites. They are calcium and limestone deposits formed by mineral-rich water that drips down the walls and ceilings of a cave. Stalagmites are similar, but they grow upwards from water dripping onto the cave floor. As long as this water seeps into the caves, the stalactites and stalagmites will form and keep growing. Sometimes, if they are very near to each other, stalactites and stalagmites join to make a column that reaches to the ceiling.

This cave is called the Big Room. It measures 540 metres from one end to the other and some columns reach 75 metres to the ceiling. Long ago, visitors to these underground caves were lowered down in buckets suspended by ropes. Today, we ride in modern lifts which take us 240 metres down to the cool, dark caverns.

4 Armadillo

As we drive through the night, across the scrubland of Edward's Plateau in Texas, we catch sight of a nine-banded armadillo in the beam of our headlights. These unusual creatures are native to southwestern USA. They are very active at night and we must slow down to avoid hitting this one as it scuttles across the road in search of insects and small reptiles.

5 Cattle Ranch

Everyone on this Texas ranch gets involved in looking after the animals. This girl is trying to lasso a longhorn cow. She practises her roping skills after school, and has been riding horses since she was three years old. Sometimes she goes out with her parents to move the cattle from one part of the ranch to another. We stay for a night, practise horseriding, and help out with the animals, too.

MUSEUM STOP

6 The Alamo, San Antonio

In 1836, when Texas was fighting for its independence from Mexico, a band of 189 volunteers was surrounded by a much bigger Mexican army. The Alamo defenders held out for two weeks until every last man was killed. 'Remember the Alamo' is still a Texan motto.

We drive along the freeway as we head towards Houston, Texas.

THE DALLAS COWBOYS

During this part of the journey we will see a famous American football team in action. The Dallas Cowboys belong to the National Football League (NFL). There are 28 teams in the NFL, and the teams are divided into the American and National Conferences. Every January the champions of both Conferences play a title game called the Super Bowl. The Dallas Cowboys won the Super Bowl in 1993.

But first we visit the Johnson Space Center, near Houston, Texas. Here, we look at rockets and other equipment used on space missions. Next, we pass some familiar structures in the Texas countryside before heading towards Dallas for an exciting game of American football. Afterwards, we try our luck hunting for diamonds in America's only public diamond field. We continue through Arkansas and learn how rice is grown in flooded fields.

OKLAHOMA
ARKANSAS
LOUISIANA
Mississippi
TEXAS

0   100 mi
0   100 km

Cheerleaders have an important job to do during a football game. They help keep both the players and supporters of their home team feeling positive and happy. The Dallas Cowboys cheerleaders are considered to be the best cheerleaders in America – and it is not easy to get into the squad. Each year thousands of young women audition for about 35 places. You have to be extremely fit and be able to learn new dance routines very quickly.

▲ Johnson Space Center

This Saturn V rocket went to the Moon and in 1973 launched the Skylab space station. As it's not busy, we are able to take a quick tour of the Mission Control Room where technicians and scientists kept in touch with the astronauts. Nearby at the Visitors' Center, we try on space helmets and touch moon rocks.

2 Oilfields

Since 1901, Texas has been famous for its oilfields. Prospectors tunnelled down using big drills, and pumps like this one are still used to bring oil to the surface. Texas now supplies the USA with a third of the oil the country needs.

3 Dallas

Texas Stadium, home of the Dallas Cowboys football team, is huge. It covers nearly 5 hectares and attracts thousands of loyal supporters.

In American football, points are scored by getting the ball across the goal line (a touchdown), or by kicking it over the crossbar, or by tackling the other team's player who has the ball in the end (safety) zone. It's a tough game and the players wear helmets and padded uniforms to protect themselves. Many of the players are large anyway, so the padding makes them look gigantic. To keep the home supporters happy, teams have squads of cheerleaders. During the game and at half-time they entertain the crowds with rhythmic cheers (shouts) and dance routines.

4 Crater of Diamonds

As in any diamond field, you will find it hard to spot a diamond 'in the rough' as they are naturally dull. Here, we discover how they have to be cut and polished to become jewels. We also learn that diamonds are the hardest substance known and can cut and grind other hard materials.

5 Rice Fields

Rice is grown in many areas of the American south. It needs plenty of heat and is the only cereal crop that must be planted and grown on very wet land. We look out for the rice fields as we travel through Arkansas. They have to be flooded regularly in order to keep the rice crop growing fast.

Next we head for the home of Dixieland jazz.

35

THE MISSISSIPPI

Before the American Civil War, some of the wealthiest Americans lived in mansions along the Mississippi River. They made their wealth by using black slaves to grow cotton. Along the giant river, Europeans, Native Americans, and Africans created a distinctive southern way of life throughout the 19th century. This southern culture, especially its music, has become famous.

Memphis, Tennessee, is well-known as the home of the 'Blues'. Elvis Presley lived here, and his home is our first stop. Then we head southwards to visit the old cotton plantation town of Vicksburg. After a trip on the Mississippi, we arrive at one of the South's great cities, New Orleans. Its fun-loving reputation has given it the nickname of 'The Big Easy'. Different cultures have merged here, giving the city its own sort of music and food. Like Montreal, New Orleans is an American city in the French style. A day out from New Orleans will take us into the swamps.

② Vicksburg

At Vicksburg a National Military Park marks the site of an important battle in the American Civil War. The hills around and Vicksburg's position beside the Mississippi made the city valuable to both sides. From it, you could control the river trade. The southern Confederates defended the city against the northern Union forces for 47 days until 4 July 1863. The local people remembered the defeat so bitterly that they refused to celebrate the 4th of July (American Independence Day) until the late 1940s.

 MUSEUM STOP

▶ **Graceland**

Elvis Presley (1935–1977) was one of the most popular singers ever. His unique voice and good looks made him a TV and film star and his fans called him the King of Rock 'n' Roll. Presley's music was influenced by many kinds of music, including southern blues, gospel, and country. As we tour Graceland we learn that he bought the mansion for $100,000 when he was only 22. In the Trophy Building we see his many awards and glittering stage costumes.

3 Mississippi Paddle-Steamer

The Mississippi River is 3,780 km long. It stretches from its source close to the Canadian border to the Gulf of Mexico. In the south it has been an important transportation route for centuries. By the 1700s, it was a vital route for European traders who shipped their goods down the river for sale in Natchez and New Orleans. But the boats used to move the goods struggled to cope with the river's strong currents. The paddle-steamer was the answer. It had a strong engine that turned a large circular paddle. Today, only tourists like us can travel on these grand old boats.

5 The Swamps

As the Mississippi River reaches the sea, it slows down and deposits much of the mud it has collected on its way. Slowly, these deposits create a swampland called a delta. We take a boat along some of the small streams called bayous, which cut through the delta and provide a home for plenty of wildlife. Bayou Teche is the largest, with rice paddies and sugar cane growing along its banks. The local Cajun people use pirogues (canoe-like boats) for fishing, and live in cabins built on stilts.

4 Jazz in New Orleans

A visit to Congo Square in New Orleans takes us to one of many jazz sites in the city. In the 1830s slaves from Africa would dance and sing on Sundays in the square, and the rhythm of their African music can still be heard in jazz music today.

Classic 'Dixieland' jazz was first performed in the many bars of the rough New Orleans' neighbourhood of Storyville. Here, famous trumpeters like Louis Armstrong began their careers. Storyville was so notorious for its drug dens and wild nightlife that the US Army closed it down in 1917. Many of the musicians left, taking jazz music to Memphis, Chicago, and New York. By the 1920s, jazz was the most popular form of American music. But New Orleans' unique mix of French, Spanish, Caribbean, African, and American influences continues to make it special. The French Quarter was planned in 1721 and still has its pretty houses with decorated balconies and colourful shutters. The St Louis Cathedral was built in 1794 under Spanish rule. You can taste Caribbean and African connections in the foods that have African names, such gumbo (a thick soup with okra and chicken) and jambalaya (rice with seafood).

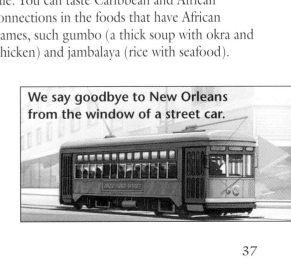

We say goodbye to New Orleans from the window of a street car.

THE CHANGING SOUTH

The South was, for many years, the land of slavery. Even after slavery was abolished here in 1863, African Americans were treated as second-class citizens. Until the 1960s they did not have an equal right to vote, and were not allowed to attend the same schools as whites or eat in the same restaurants. Although problems remain, there are now black mayors and millionaires in the South.

On this part of our journey we take a look at America's history from the Civil War to civil rights. We visit a Civil War battlefield and tour a Second World War battleship. We also learn about a man whose belief in peaceful protest cost him his life. Then, for some fun, we go to Atlanta and watch a baseball game between the Atlanta Braves and Detroit Tigers, before heading further south towards the Okefenokee Swamp in southeastern Georgia.

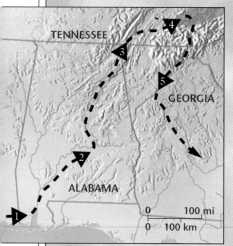

ⅢⅢ MUSEUM STOP

▼ Battleship Park

Battleship Park at Mobile Bay is home to a Second World War battleship, the *USS Alabama*. It was attacked by Kamikaze pilots (Japanese suicide-bombers) who tried to crash into it and other warships from the Allied countries. Anchored alongside is the *USS Drum*, a Second World War submarine that we can tour. Some people feel uncomfortable walking through its small, tight compartments.

▼ Montgomery

In early 1861, Alabama's domed Capitol building in Montgomery served as the headquarters of the Confederacy, the government established by the Southern states during the Civil War. Inside, murals decorate the walls and a bronze star marks the spot where Jefferson Davis was sworn in as the Confederacy's first (and only) president.

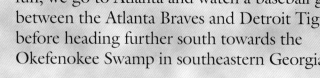

▼ Chattanooga Military Park

In November 1863, in nearby woods, the bloodiest battle of the Civil War took place. Of the 120,000 men who fought, over 35,000 were killed, wounded, or went missing. This is America's oldest military park and we see many monuments during our walk. We also take a ride on the world's steepest incline railway to the top of Lookout Mountain.

INFORMATION PACK

Born in Atlanta, Martin Luther King Jr was a devout Christian who led African Americans in a non-violent struggle to achieve equal rights. Until the 1960s, blacks were not allowed the same use of public services as whites. For example, they were not allowed to sit next to whites on Montgomery's buses and even had to give up their seats to them. King was murdered for his beliefs in Memphis in 1968 but many of his goals were achieved and his memory continues to inspire.

4 ▶ Great Smoky Mountains

In this region we spot a wild boar. European wild boar were brought here by sportsmen in the early 1900s. Many of the boar escaped their enclosures and bred in the wild. Unfortunately their feeding activity is damaging the ecosystem. As they root in the soil they speed-up erosion. They also make it more difficult for native wildlife to find food.

5 ▼ Atlanta

Atlanta has a modern skyline and a dynamic African-American community. Sporting events play a big part in city life. In 1996, Atlanta hosted the Olympic games. Here at Turner Field, the Braves are playing against the Detroit Tigers. The Braves won baseball's National League Championship several times throughout the 1990s.

We ride past peanut fields on our way south.

THE EVERGLADES

This vast marshland covers over half a million hectares of southwest Florida. It is a very important habitat for many endangered animal species, including the Florida panther and the West Indian manatee. For many years the Everglades have been under threat from pollution caused by bad farming practices and housing developments, but restrictions are in place and campaigns continue to protect this beautiful wilderness.

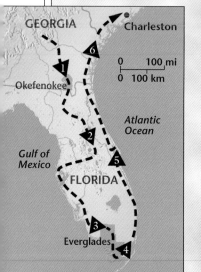

We begin with a visit to Okefenokee Swamp. Until the 1850s, the swamp was a refuge from white settlers for the Seminole Native Americans. Next, we take a trip to Disney World before heading south to the Everglades. From there, we go to Miami Beach before visiting the Kennedy Space Center for a look at space travel, past and present. Finally, in Savannah, Georgia, we see a building that was once devoted to the thriving cotton industry.

2 Walt Disney World

Walt Disney World attracts nearly 120,000 visitors each day. Although it is one of the main theme parks at Walt Disney World, the EPCOT Center has little to do with Mickey Mouse and fairy tales. Our EPCOT train takes us to Future World. Inside the glass geosphere we learn how farming, travelling, and communicating might work in the future.

3 Everglades National Park

This huge subtropical wilderness of flat, grassy swamp and woodland supports many endangered animals such as the Atlantic Hawksbill turtle. During the summer, heavy rain floods much of the Everglades causing wildlife to retreat to pine forests and hammocks. Hammocks are dense groupings of hardwood trees, such as oak and red maple, that grow on slightly raised land near the swamp. Cypress trees grow directly in the water surrounding the hammocks. From the safety of the boardwalk we watch some alligators keeping cool in the water. Alligators feed mainly on fish, frogs, and small mammals.

1 Okefenokee Swamp

'Okefenokee' means 'trembling earth' and you find, when you step onto the soft, peat-based islands, that they do move gently. The area is an important habitat for many wading birds and mammals. We take a speedboat across the swamp and see otters bobbing in and out of the water in search of shellfish and amphibians. We come upon rare storks and herons, including these blue herons, fishing along the muddy banks.

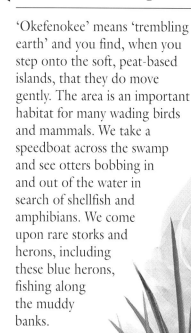

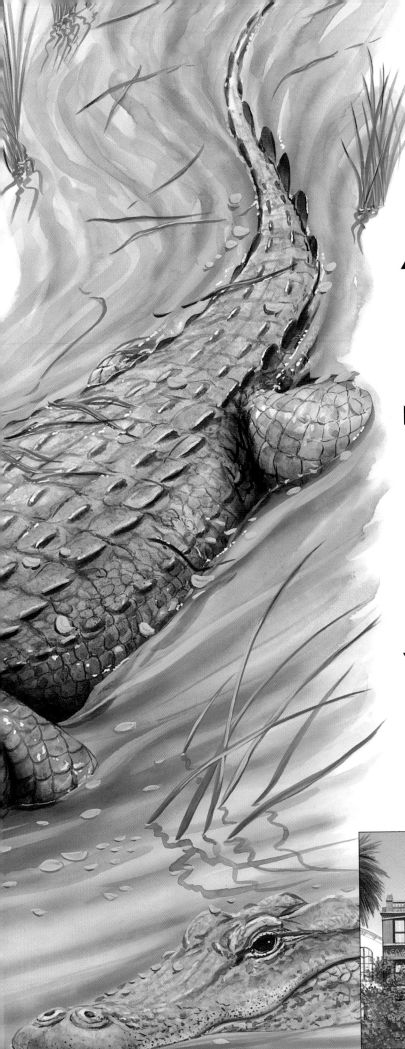

4 Miami Beach

Miami Beach is famous for its palm trees and stylish houses and hotels. The beaches attracted the rich and famous in the 1950s. Their luxury mansions drew thousands of ordinary tourists to the resort. At the same time, a revolution in Cuba produced an inflow of refugees. Now the vast majority of Miami's one million Spanish-speaking residents are Cuban.

5 Kennedy Space Center

The early space launches took place across the water at Cape Canaveral US Air Force base. The larger, later rockets were launched from the Kennedy Space Center, on Merritt Island. At the Space Center there are eight genuine rockets. After viewing these we go on board a full-sized replica of the *Explorer* Space Shuttle.

6 Savannah

In the 1800s, cotton was grown throughout the Deep South. Savannah, a busy seaport, dealt with the transportation of the cotton to mills around the world. On our walk through the town we see the Cotton Exchange where brokers set the prices.

We take a carriage ride through Charleston to our next stop.

41

THE SOUTHERN PLANTATIONS

Cotton, rice, and tobacco were the main crops grown on the Southern plantations during the 18th and 19th centuries. The plantation owners wanted to be self-sufficient, growing food crops and making their own clothes, furniture, and tools. Some of their slaves were hired out to other employers, making their owners rich. In 1776, the richest men in the USA were South Carolinian slave-owners.

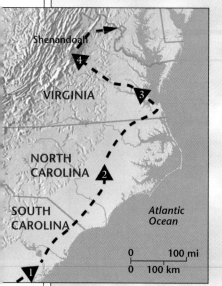

We begin this part of our journey near Charleston, South Carolina, with a tour of Drayton Hall. This mansion is one of the few plantation houses to have survived the Civil War. Next, we pass the tobacco fields of North Carolina as we head north into Virginia. At Colonial Williamsburg we experience a day of 18th-century life. Finally, we travel along Skyline Drive, the backbone of the Blue Ridge Mountains, and set up camp for the night.

MUSEUM STOP

Drayton Hall

Drayton Hall is the only mansion on the Ashley River to have survived the devastation of the Civil War. We learn about the slaves who were brought from West Africa to grow rice, a major crop in the South. They also wove baskets from the reeds that grew along the riverside.

2 Tobacco Fields

Our journey takes us on past many tobacco fields. North Carolina is a major producer of cigarettes. Its warm climate and fertile soil provide ideal conditions for the tobacco plant. It is now known that smoking tobacco leads to illnesses such as cancer, but many people find it difficult to stop smoking.

3 Colonial Williamsburg

Williamsburg was the capital of Virginia until 1776. Famous American politicians, including US presidents George Washington and Thomas Jefferson, began their political careers here.

Much of Williamsburg was ruined during the Revolutionary War, but what was left was bought and preserved during the 1920s. Many buildings have been restored and others have been carefully reconstructed to make Colonial Williamsburg America's largest historical theme park. People dressed in colonial costume walk along the streets of the town. We see soldiers, some playing pipes and drums, marching along. Cars are banned from the area, so all our touring is done on foot and by bicycle. (If you get tired and hungry, there are several 18th-century taverns for you to sit down and eat in.) We visit some original workshops and watch craftsmen, including silversmiths, blacksmiths, and candlemakers, work as they would have done 200 years ago. Next, we visit the courthouse where several of Blackbeard's pirates were put on trial. Lastly, we tour an octagonal (eight-sided) ammunition store.

4 Shenandoah National Park

While camping here in the Blue Ridge Mountains, we hear rustling noises outside our tent. Carefully, we unzip our tent and shine a torch towards the noise. It is an opossum, in search of food. When frightened, opossums lie still, pretending to be dead.

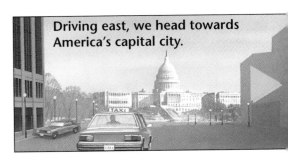

Driving east, we head towards America's capital city.

THE CAPITOL BUILDING

We have reached America's capital, Washington D.C. From the tidy lawns of the Mall in the city centre we get a good view of the Capitol Building. There is usually something important taking place here. The nation's law-makers gather here to discuss and debate how money will be spent and which laws should be passed. It is also where the president entertains members of royalty and foreign presidents.

We first take a brisk tour of the city itself, beginning with the White House. The Capitol Building is our next stop, where we watch Congress at work. As we walk past the Vietnam Veterans Memorial we see people search for the names of relatives who were killed during the Vietnam War. We then leave Washington for Lancaster County, Pennsylvania. For our last stop, we travel east to America's first capital city, Philadelphia. We leave North America from New York Harbor. Our last view is of the Manhattan skyline and the twin towers of the World Trade Center.

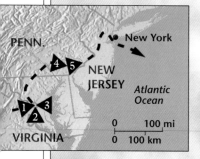

2 Capitol Building

The US Congress meets at the Capitol Building to debate national issues. Congress is divided into the House of Representatives and the Senate. The House controls spending and the Senate approves foreign treaties. Both houses have to pass laws. Inside we can watch the House or Senate debate from the public galleries.

The Capitol Building was nearly destroyed by the British during an invasion in 1814 but was renovated by 1819. Its iron dome weighs an amazing 4 million kilograms. The ceiling is painted with a picture of George Washington being welcomed into heaven by thirteen angels who represent the original thirteen states of America. Later artists have painted pictures of America's great heroes onto the walls and ceiling. The most recent one is of the *Challenger* Space Shuttle astronauts.

1 The White House

The White House, at 1600 Pennsylvania Avenue, has been home to every president since 1801. The president works from the Oval Office and is photographed with important visitors in the Rose Garden. We are able to see eight rooms in the White House including the China Room, which is filled with beautiful pottery.

3 ▸ Arlington

Arlington National Cemetery is the official burial site for those who have died in the service of the United States. It includes the graves of President Kennedy and his brother Robert. Outside the cemetery there is a dramatic statue of soldiers raising the US flag. This honours the marines who fought against the Japanese in World War II. From Arlington we look across the Potomac river and see the Washington and Lincoln memorials.

4 ▸ Lancaster County

In Pennsylvania, we visit an Amish community. The Amish people choose not to have televisions, computers, cars, or many of the things that most of us take for granted. They grow their own food, build their own houses, and have their own schools. Their clothing is plain and, like many aspects of their lives, the style has hardly changed since they first arrived in Lancaster County during the 1720s. They came here from Switzerland, where they were not allowed to practise the form of Christianity that they believe in.

5 ▸ Philadelphia

Philadelphia was America's first capital and was founded in 1682 by the English Quaker William Penn. By 1776, many non-Quakers lived in Pennsylvania and wanted independence from Britain and an end to the power of the Penn family. We take time to visit Liberty Bell, which was hung in Independence Hall and rang out American victories during the Revolutionary War.

We say goodbye from the deck of a cruise ship.

INDEX